Water: Concepts and Applications
Introduction

Organization

Water: Concepts and Applications serves as a companion to the regular science curriculum. It is divided into three units: Concepts; Uses and Importance; and Effects on the Environment. Each unit contains concise background information on the unit's topics, as well as activities to reinforce students' knowledge and understanding of basic principles of water.

Introduction

This book contains three types of pages:

- Concise background information is provided for each unit. These pages are intended for the parent's or teacher's use. Important vocabulary words are included on these pages. Some information on the student assessments comes from these pages.

- Assessments are included to test students' understanding of the concepts. These are meant to be reproduced.

- Activity pages list the materials and steps necessary for students to complete projects. Questions for students to answer are also included on these pages. As much as possible, these activities include most of the multiple intelligences so students can use their strengths to achieve a well-balanced learning style. These pages are also meant for reproduction for use by all students.

Use

Water: Concepts and Applications is designed for independent use by students who have been introduced to the skills and concepts described. This book is a means to supplement the regular science curriculum; it is not meant to replace it. Copies of the activities can be given to individuals, pairs of students, or small groups for completion. They may also be used as a center activity. If the students are familiar with the content, the worksheets may also be sent home as homework.

The following plan suggests a format to implement these activities.

1. Explain the purpose of the worksheets to your students. Let them know that these activities will be fun as well as helpful.

2. Review the mechanics of how you want the students to work with the activities. Do you want them to work in groups? Are the activities for homework?

3. Decide how you would like to use the assessments. They can be given before and after a unit to determine progress, or only after a unit to assess how well the concepts have been learned. Determine whether you will send the tests home or keep them in the students' portfolios.

4. Introduce the students to the process and purpose of the activities. Go over the directions together. Work with the students when they have difficulty. Work only a few pages at a time to ensure success.

5. Do a practice activity together.

FOSS Correlation

The Full Option Science System™ (FOSS) was developed at the University of California at Berkeley. It is a coordinated science curriculum organized into four categories: Life Science, Physical Science, Earth Science, and Scientific Reasoning & Technology. Under each category are various modules that span two grade levels. The module for the grade level featured in this book is highlighted in the chart below.

FOSS

Water	8, 17, 18, 19, 20, 21, 23, 24, 26, 28, 30

Curriculum Correlation

Social Studies	28
Math	9, 10, 12, 13, 14, 23, 25, 27, 29
Science	11, 21
Language Arts	10, 17, 25, 27, 29

D1469361

General Background

Water

Water is our most precious resource. Water covers about 70 percent of the Earth's surface in the forms of rivers, lakes, seas, and oceans. Without water, life could not exist. Our bodies are about 65 percent water. We use water in many ways. Water is a powerful source of energy. It can also change the Earth's surface through **weathering** and **erosion**.

Water is an amazing substance. It can be a **solid**, a **liquid**, and a **gas**. It can change from a solid state (ice) to a liquid state (water) to a gaseous state (water vapor) and back again.

Water as a solid is good for cooling and preserving things, and for fun and recreation. Have you ever had a cold glass of ice water on a hot day? Have you ever been ice-skating? Then you have used water as a solid.

Water as a gas is perhaps its most interesting form. Water as a gas is called **water vapor**. The amount of water vapor in the air is called **humidity**. Different air masses have different levels of humidity. Air, depending on its temperature, can only hold so much humidity. When too much humidity is in the air, some of it is released in the form of precipitation.

There are many forms of precipitation. For example, the drops of water on grass in the cool morning are a form of **precipitation**. These drops are called dew. When the air is cold enough, these drops become frost. Other kinds of precipitation are rain, snow, sleet, hail, and fog.

Water is a valuable resource that we all need to work hard to protect. If our water becomes polluted, then many plants, animals, and people will suffer. We need to do our part to keep rivers, lakes, and oceans clean so that we can enjoy them. Once our water is polluted, it is very hard to clean it and make it safe to drink or use.

Water

Directions ➡ Read each sentence. Write **T** if the statement is true, or **F** if the statement is false.

_____ **1.** Evaporation occurs when liquid water is frozen.

_____ **2.** Water has no odor or taste.

_____ **3.** When water turns to ice, it changes states from a liquid to a solid.

_____ **4.** Matter cannot change states.

_____ **5.** Grass and trees keep the wind from blowing away the soil.

Directions ➡ Read each sentence. Circle the letter of the answer that best completes each sentence.

6. _____ is a part of the water cycle.
  A. Weather
  B. Precipitation
  C. Tornado

7. _____ is a state of matter.
  A. Solid
  B. Liquid
  C. Both **A** and **B**

8. _____ is the gaseous form of water.
  A. Ice
  B. Water vapor
  C. Rain

9. Moving water has _____.
  A. salt
  B. electricity
  C. energy

10. When ocean water evaporates, _____ is left behind.
  A. salt
  B. ice
  C. rain

11. _____ is the breaking down and carrying away of rocks and soil.
  A. Evaporation
  B. Watering
  C. Erosion

Go on to the next page.

Water, p. 2

Directions → Match each term with the correct statement. Write the letter of the term on the line.

_____ **12.** This is the process of water changing from its liquid form to its gaseous form and back to its liquid form.

A. dam

B. ocean

_____ **13.** This is a state of matter.

_____ **14.** This holds back water.

C. hard

_____ **15.** Three fourths of the Earth is covered by this kind of water.

D. pond

_____ **16.** Water is this if it has a lot of matter dissolved in it.

E. water cycle

_____ **17.** This forms when water collects in a low-lying area.

F. delta

_____ **18.** This forms at the mouth of a river and has fertile soil.

G. gas

Directions → Answer each question in a complete sentence.

19. What does erosion do to the Earth's surface? _____

_____

_____

20. How do rivers form? _____

_____

Water: Concepts and Applications, Gr. 3, SV 2709-X

The Water Cycle

Water often changes from its liquid form to its gaseous form and back to its liquid form in a process called the **water cycle**. The three main steps in the water cycle are **evaporation**, **condensation**, and **precipitation**. Evaporation is necessary to get the liquid water into its gaseous form of water vapor in the air. Condensation is needed to turn the vapor back to a liquid in the clouds. And precipitation returns the liquid water to the Earth.

Evaporation occurs as liquid water is heated and changed into water vapor. The water vapor is then carried up into the sky by rising air. Condensation takes place as the rising water vapor cools and is changed into liquid water, forming clouds. Precipitation happens as water droplets grow heavy and fall to the Earth as rain, snow, or some other type of precipitation.

Matter

Matter is all around. It is everything that we see and touch. Moreover, matter has **mass**, or weight, and takes up space. Matter is identified in three forms—**solid**, **liquid**, and **gas**.

All matter is made up of tiny particles called **molecules**. Molecules are made up of even smaller particles called **atoms**. Molecules cannot be seen with a microscope, but students can understand a substance's properties by using their senses when performing simple experiments.

Solids

The state of matter is determined by the density of the molecules and how fast they move. In a solid, the molecules are attracted to each other and are tightly held together. The movement of the particles is limited—they vibrate only. Therefore, a solid has a definite shape and volume. For example, a rock has a certain shape. It can be broken into smaller pieces, but its molecules do not change. A solid's mass is measured in **grams** (g), a metric weight that is a scientific measurement standard.

Liquids

Liquids have a definite volume, but they take the shape of the container. The molecules in a liquid are not packed as tightly, so they can move about more freely and easily by sliding over each other. This movement is what makes a liquid take the shape of the container. When water is in a pitcher, it takes the shape of the pitcher. Yet if poured into a glass, the water takes the shape of the glass. The volume of a liquid is measured in **milliliters** (**mL**), the scientific standard measurement for liquid.

Gas

Gas is the third state of matter. It is harder for students to understand the properties of gas, because they cannot see it, nor have they had any exposure to different kinds of gases. In a gas, the molecules are far apart and move very quickly and randomly in all directions. They bounce off of each other when they collide. Gas has no definite shape or volume. Gas, therefore, expands to take the shape of a container. Gas is also measured in milliliters (mL).

Matter Changes

All matter can change form, meaning it can change from one state to another. When matter changes, nothing is lost or gained—the molecules stay the same. The addition or the removal of heat causes the molecules to get closer or farther apart. Moreover, the greater the amount of heat, the faster the molecules move. These changes in the density and the speed of a substance's molecules cause the state of matter to change.

Students can easily experiment with changes in states by watching ice change to water and steam. Ice is a solid, but when heated to its freezing point, turns to liquid water. No water is lost or gained in the process, and no molecules are changed. When more heat is added, the water changes to a gas called **water vapor** when it reaches its boiling point. The gas cannot be seen, because it has no color. Again, no water is lost or gained, and the molecules stay the same. If a spoon is held in the water vapor, the surface temperature of the spoon, which is room temperature, causes the water vapor to cool and condense back to liquid water. Likewise, by removing the heat and freezing the water, it changes states again to become ice.

Unit 1 Assessment

Directions → Match each term with the correct statement. Write the letter of the term on the line.

_____ 1. This is the process of water changing from its liquid form to its gaseous form and back to its liquid form.

_____ 2. This is what water is in its gaseous form.

_____ 3. Water becomes this when it changes from a liquid to a solid.

_____ 4. This can change states.

_____ 5. Heat makes liquids do this.

A. matter

B. evaporate

C. water vapor

D. water cycle

E. ice

Directions → Use the terms to complete the statements. Write the terms on the lines.

Condensation   Water   Earth   Heat   Precipitation

6. _____ takes place as rising water vapor cools and changes into liquid water.

7. _____ happens as water droplets grow heavy and fall to the Earth as rain, sleet, or snow.

8. _____ has no odor or taste.

9. _____ is either added or removed to cause state changes in matter.

10. _____ is covered 70 percent by water.

Unit 1 The Water Cycle

Water often changes from its liquid form to its gaseous form and back to its liquid form in a process called the **water cycle**. The three main steps in the water cycle are **evaporation, condensation**, and **precipitation**. Evaporation is necessary to get the liquid water into its gaseous form of water vapor in the air. Condensation is needed to turn the vapor back to a liquid in the clouds. And precipitation returns the liquid water to the Earth.

Evaporation occurs as liquid water is heated and changed into water vapor. The water vapor is then carried up into the sky by rising air. Condensation takes place as the rising water vapor cools and is changed into liquid water, forming clouds. Precipitation happens as water droplets grow heavy and fall to the Earth as rain, snow, or sleet. Water is constantly moving back and forth from the air to the ground in the water cycle.

Directions ➞ Label the steps of the water cycle in the picture below. Write **evaporation, condensation**, or **precipitation** on the correct line.

Unit 1

Water Facts

Water has no odor or taste. Below 0° C, it is solid ice. It is hard and cold, and it can float on liquid water. From 0° C to 100° C, water is a liquid. It pours and flows. Above 100° C, water is a gas called water vapor. Water vapor cannot be seen.

In its solid and liquid forms, water covers about 70 percent of the surface of the Earth. Water is in the air, too. Much of the time it is invisible water vapor. Often, however, water vapor in the air changes form. Then you can see it as clouds, rain, fog, snow, hail, or sleet, or as dew or frost on plants and cars.

Most of your body is water. Water makes up 92 percent of the liquid part of your blood. It makes up 80 percent of your muscles. You need water to live. A person can live without water for only 7 to 10 days.

Directions → **Read each sentence. Write T if the statement is true, or F if the statement is false.**

_____ **1.** Ice floats on liquid water.

_____ **2.** Water forms a gas at 0° C.

_____ **3.** Water vapor in the air may become frost.

_____ **4.** You can see water vapor.

_____ **5.** A person can live without water for a month.

Unit 1

From Water to Ice

When water turns to ice, it changes state. It changes from a liquid to a solid. Does the weight of the water change, too?

MATERIALS	balloon	water	scale	freezer

Try This:

A. Over a sink or basin, fill the balloon with water. Tie the open end into a tight knot.

B. Place the water-filled balloon on a scale.

What does it weigh? _____

C. Put the water-filled balloon in the freezer. Leave it overnight. When all the water in the balloon has turned to ice, place the balloon on the scale.

What does it weigh? _____

Directions → Answer the questions.

1. The water in the balloon changed from liquid to solid form. Did the

weight of the water change? _____

2. How do you explain what happened? _____

_____

_____

Unit 1 — From Solid to Liquid

Matter can change states. Solids can become liquids, and liquids can change to solids. How does this happen? Heat is either added to or removed from matter to cause state changes. Think about an ice cube. If you hold it in your hand, it gets warmer and begins to melt (becomes a liquid). However, if you put water in a freezer, it freezes (becomes a solid).

MATERIALS
ice cubes
small self-sealing plastic bag
watch or clock

Try This:

A. Think of ways to make ice cubes melt quickly.
Choose the idea that you think is best.

B. Place an ice cube in the bag. Try your idea.
Use a watch or clock to time it.

C. Write the time it took to melt the ice cube. Compare
your time with the times of some of your classmates.

Directions ➞ **Answer the questions.**

1. How long did it take your ice cube to melt?

_____

2. What made the ice cube melt? _____

3. What was the quickest way you found to melt an ice cube?

_____

_____

From Liquid to Gas

Remember, matter can change states. Think about what happens when you climb out of a swimming pool on a hot day. You leave wet footprints as you walk across the cement. The liquid water evaporates to become water vapor in the air. If you cool the air, water vapor condenses on objects such as grass and leaves. In this experiment, you will see how heat makes liquids evaporate.

MATERIALS
2 paper towels
1 glass of water

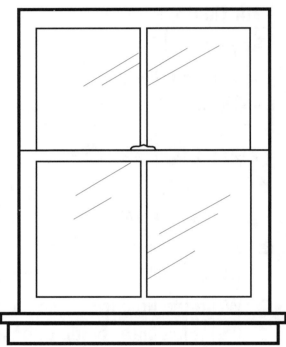

Try This:

A. Sprinkle water on the paper towels. Do not put a lot of water on them.

B. Place 1 towel in a cool, dark place. Place the other on a sunny windowsill.

C. Every few minutes, check to see if the towels are dry.

Directions ➞ **Answer the questions.**

1. Which towel was dry first? _____

2. Why did this towel dry first? _____

_____

3. Where did the water in the towel go? _____

_____

Name _____   Date _____

How Long Did It Take?

If you leave a cup of water out long enough, the water will all evaporate. What happens if you pour the same amount of water into a pie tin or a soda bottle? Does it take the same amount of time to evaporate? Does it take more or less time?

MATERIALS		
large paper cup	pie tin	measuring cup
soda bottle	funnel	water

Try This:

A. Put the paper cup, the pie tin, and the soda bottle on a table where they can stay for a week. Make sure they are out of direct sunlight and away from drafts. Fill the measuring cup with water. The cup holds 250 milliliters. Pour the water into the paper cup.

B. Pour 1 measuring cup of water into a pie tin. Using the funnel, pour 1 measuring cup of water into the soda bottle.

C. The next day, carefully pour the water from the paper cup into the measuring cup. Record the water level in the graph on the next page. Pour the water back into the paper cup.

D. Do the same thing with the water in the soda bottle. Use the funnel when you pour the water back into the bottle.

E. Ask your teacher to help you pour the water from the pie tin into the measuring cup. Record your measurements in the graph.

F. Every day for a week, measure the water left in each container. Record your results.

Go on to the next page.

How Long Did It Take?, p. 2

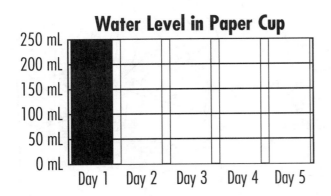

Water Level in Paper Cup

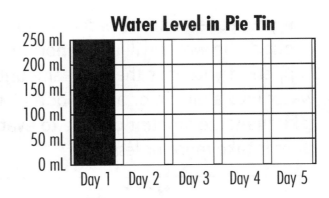

Water Level in Pie Tin

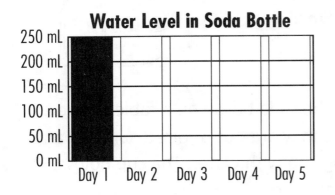

Water Level in Soda Bottle

Directions → **Answer the questions.**

1. Did the water evaporate most quickly from the paper cup, pie tin, or

soda bottle? _____

How long did it take? _____

2. From which of the 3 containers did the water evaporate most slowly?

_____

3. How can you explain your results? _____

_____

_____

Unit 1: Concepts
Water: Concepts and Applications, Gr. 3, SV 2709-X

Sources of Energy

Energy is the ability to move things. We can see that the wind has energy when it blows a tree and that water has energy when it moves a boat. The force of the wind or water is being transferred to the object being moved. The more force exerted, the faster and farther it will go.

Technology has found ways to harness all these different kinds of energy so that they produce electricity. **Electricity** is the energy that flows through wires. Power plants that produce electricity often use a variety of energy sources, such as water or fuels, to produce electricity.

Water is a good conductor of electricity. All electrical appliances need to be kept away from water, including rain. An electric shock is the result when the water and electricity interact. The contact could result in your immediate death. Electricity is an important part of life, but it can be dangerous if you do not use it carefully.

Water

Moving water has energy. In grain mills long ago, people discovered that the moving water transferred its energy to turn wheels. That energy then traveled to other wheels that would grind the grain. Modern technology has capitalized on this process and developed ways to utilize large amounts of water energy. Huge **power plants** use the movement of water to turn large wheels, called **turbines**, which run generators to produce electricity. The water energy is transferred to electric energy to produce electricity for houses.

Stored water has energy, too. As water is released from the elevated storage tank, the force of gravity pulls the water downward. The force of the stored water provides energy. A **dam** holds, or stores, water, but when released, the water pours through the gates with great force. The force of the water is transferred to anything that is in its path.

Assessment

Directions → Read each sentence. Circle the letter of the answer that best completes each sentence.

1. _____ is needed for drinking, cleaning, and keeping us cool.
  A. Oxygen
  B. Dirt
  C. Water

2. Our _____ are about two thirds water.
  A. houses
  B. bodies
  C. bones

3. A _____ holds back water.
  A. bridge
  B. mountain
  C. dam

4. Moving water has _____.
  A. energy
  B. electricity
  C. a charge

Directions → Read each sentence. Write **T** if the sentence is true, or **F** if the sentence is false.

_____ **5.** Plants and animals can live without water.

_____ **6.** You can use salty water to water plants and to drink.

_____ **7.** Matter can dissolve in water.

_____ **8.** Ocean water is salty.

_____ **9.** Hard water has a lot of matter dissolved in it.

10. What are three reasons we need water? _____

_____

_____

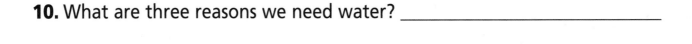

2 Water on the Earth

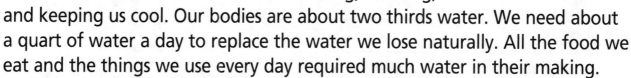

    Every day we take many things for granted. One thing we take for granted is water. No plant or animal could live without water. It is needed for drinking, cleaning, and keeping us cool. Our bodies are about two thirds water. We need about a quart of water a day to replace the water we lose naturally. All the food we eat and the things we use every day required much water in their making.

    Americans use a half trillion gallons of water a day. Each person in the United States uses about 90 gallons of water a day for cleaning and gardening. Two more gallons per person are used for drinking and cooking. Factories use lots of water to make goods. It takes 60,000 gallons of water to make one ton of steel. Farmers use 115 gallons of water to grow the wheat for one loaf of bread, and 4,000 gallons are needed to get 1 pound of beef. As you can see, water is very important to us all. We must always be sure to take care of the water we have.

Directions ➡ **Answer the questions.**

1. What three things do humans use water for?

_____

2. How much of our bodies is water?

_____

3. How much water do people need to drink in 1 day?

_____

4. How many gallons of water do Americans use in 1 day?

_____

5. How many gallons does it take to make 1 loaf of bread?

_____

Unit 2 The Energy of Water

A dam holds back water. When the water moves, it has energy. Try this experiment to see how a dam works.

MATERIALS	
clean milk carton	water
scissors	pinwheel

Try This:

A. Cut off 1 side of a milk carton. Keep the piece in 1 large strip.

B. Cut a hole in the bottom of the carton.

C. Place the large strip behind the hole. Press it so it is snug. Hold it in place.

D. Have a friend help you. Hold the milk carton over a sink. Fill it with water. Press against the large strip to keep in the water.

E. Have your friend hold the pinwheel under the dam.

Directions → Answer the questions.

1. Does the pinwheel turn? _____

2. Now pull out the strip. What happens? _____

_____

Moving water has energy. It can turn a small pinwheel. It can also turn large wheels in machines that produce electric energy. The energy of water moving through a dam can be changed to electric energy.

© Steck-Vaughn Company

Unit 2: Uses and Importance
Water: Concepts and Applications, Gr. 3, SV 2709-X

Using the Ocean Water

Nearly three fourths of the Earth is covered by ocean water. Nine tenths of this water is salty. You cannot drink salty water. You cannot use it for watering plants, either. How could you get the salt out of water so that it could be used? Try this activity to find out how.

MATERIALS
pie pan   salt   water
tablespoon   1 cup measure
glass bowl smaller than the pan
clear plastic mixing bowl that will fit over the glass bowl

Try This:

A. Mix a tablespoon of salt and a cup of water. Pour the salt water into the small bowl.

B. Place the small glass bowl in the pie pan.

C. Cover the bowl with the larger mixing bowl, and place it in the sunlight for a few hours.

Directions ➡ **Answer the questions.**

1. Taste the water in the pan. Does it contain salt? _____

2. Taste the water in the small bowl. Does it contain salt? _____

3. Explain how the salt and the water were separated.

_____

_____

_____

Unit 2 Is Your Water Hard or Soft?

Matter such as salt can dissolve in water. All tap water has some matter dissolved in it. If water has a lot of matter dissolved in it, it is called **hard water**. Water with only a little matter dissolved in it is called **soft water**.

MATERIALS
rainwater or distilled water
liquid soap
2 jars with lids
$\frac{1}{4}$ teaspoon measure

Try This:

A. Put a cup of rainwater in 1 jar. Rainwater is soft. It has no matter dissolved in it. Put a cup of tap water in the other jar.

B. Put exactly one $\frac{1}{4}$ teaspoon of soap into each jar.

C. Cover and shake each jar. Lots of suds is a sign of soft water.

Directions ➡ **Answer the questions.**

1. Did you get suds in both jars? _____

2. Do you have hard or soft water? _____

_____

The Earth's Surface Changes

The Earth's surface undergoes constant change. Some of this change is very slow and gradual. Other changes are rapid and violent. This section will look at the slow processes of weathering and erosion.

Weathering

Any process that causes rocks or landforms to break down is called **weathering**. Weathering is caused by several agents, including water, wind, ice, and plants. Weathering is usually a slow process, causing the gradual deterioration of the rocks or landforms.

Water can freeze in the cracks of rocks and cause the rocks to break apart. Plant roots can grow into rocks and cause the rocks to break into smaller parts. These are examples of **physical weathering**.

Certain chemicals can act on rocks, too. This process is called **chemical weathering**. Have you ever seen the unusual shapes in caves? These shapes are the result of the chemical weathering of limestone by water. As rainwater seeps through the soil, it can absorb carbon dioxide. The carbon dioxide turns the water into a weak acidic solution called carbonic acid. This acid dissolves the limestone. As the limestone-rich water drips, it begins to harden again, forming **stalagmites** and **stalactites**.

Erosion

Erosion is another way in which rocks and landforms are broken down or worn away. Erosion is the process in which weathered rock and soil are moved from one place to another. The most effective agents of erosion are moving water, waves, gravity, wind, and glaciers.

Moving water can change the appearance of the landscape, sometimes slowly, sometimes quickly. The Grand Canyon is an example of slow erosion caused by moving water. The frequent mudslides in California are an example of rapid erosion caused by moving water. Waves, too, can carry rocks and sand along a beach, eroding it and changing its appearance.

Gravity can pull weathered rock and soil down a hillside. The wind can pick up large amounts of sand or dust and then deposit it miles away. The great Dust Bowl in Oklahoma and other parts of the Midwest is an example of erosion by the wind.

Glaciers are great moving sheets of ice. Glaciers can pick up soil, rocks, and even boulders and then carry them for miles. These rocks and boulders scrape away at the landscape as the glacier moves over it, leaving deep gouges. The Great Lakes were formed through erosion by glaciers.

Water: Concepts and Applications, Gr. 3, SV 2709-X

Assessment

Directions ➡ Read each statement. Decide which form of water or landform the statement is describing. If it describes a pond, write **P**. If it describes a delta, write **D**. If it describes a river, write **R**.

_____ **1.** The V-shaped area at the mouth of a river.

_____ **2.** This forms when water collects in a low-lying area.

_____ **3.** It begins as melting snow or falling rain runs down a mountain.

_____ **4.** When it flows fast, it digs out new channels, which changes its shape.

_____ **5.** This is a very fertile area.

_____ **6.** Ranchers or farmers may build these for their animals' drinking water.

_____ **7.** This forms when streams join together.

_____ **8.** This flows into an ocean, a bay, or a gulf.

Directions ➡ Answer the questions in complete sentences.

9. What are some ways to reduce and prevent erosion?

_____

_____

10. How can harmful bacteria pollute water?

_____

_____

Unit 3 How Are Rocks Broken Down?

Rocks change and break. Breaking of rocks into pieces is called **weathering**. One way weathering occurs is when rainwater and carbon-dioxide gas mix in the air. The water falls to the ground and goes into cracks. The rainwater makes the rocks break. Try this experiment to see how rocks are broken down.

MATERIALS	
3 small jars	vinegar
3 labels	limestone rocks
drinking straw	crayon or pen
water	

Try This:

A. Fill 2 jars half full of water. Label 1 jar *Water*.

B. Blow through the straw into the second jar of water. The air you blow out contains carbon-dioxide gas. Label this jar *Carbon-Dioxide*.

C. Fill the third jar half full of vinegar. Label this jar *Vinegar*.

D. Put some limestone rocks in each jar. Keep 1 rock set aside.

E. Look at the jars tomorrow. Record your observations on the chart on page 24.

Go on to the next page.

How Are Rocks Broken Down?, p. 2

Directions → Fill in the chart, and answer the questions.

JAR	CHANGES IN ROCKS
Water	
Carbon dioxide	
Vinegar	

Observation

1. What changes do you see in the rocks?

_____

_____

_____

_____

Conclusion

2. How did the vinegar, the carbon dioxide, and the water change the rocks?

_____

_____

_____

_____

_____

Unit 3 Erosion

What if rain and wind washed all the rocks and soil away? Would you be able to grow plants? Would your home be safe? Could you travel safely on roads and highways?

Erosion is the breaking down and carrying away of rocks and soil. How can erosion be stopped? Bushes and trees can be planted. The roots grow into the soil and keep it from being washed and blown away. Leaves fall on the soil and make a cover that protects the soil. Grass can be planted in sandy soil. The grass keeps the wind from blowing the soil away. Along roads and hillsides, crushed rock or bark can be used to cover the soil. This keeps the soil in place when it rains.

Directions ➡ **Look at the pairs of pictures. Circle the picture in each pair that shows a way of stopping erosion. On your own paper, write a sentence about how erosion is being stopped in each picture you circled.**

1. a. 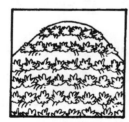   **b.**    **2. a.**    **b.**

3. a.    **b.** 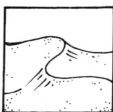   **4. a.**    **b.**

Unit 3: Effects on the Environment
Water: Concepts and Applications, Gr. 3, SV 2709-X

Unit 3 How Ponds Form and Change

How does a puddle form? After a rain, most of the water that has fallen flows down into the ground or into a storm sewer. But if a tree branch blocks the water's path, a puddle can form. Or if there's a low area in a sidewalk or a field, the water will form a puddle there, too. In the same way that puddles form, ponds can also form.

Although puddles form accidentally, beavers often work to form ponds. Beavers spend much of their time building and taking care of their dams. These dams keep the water in a stream from flowing along its natural course. As the water builds up behind the dam, a pond forms.

People build ponds for many reasons. Some people build ponds to have a place for swimming. Ranchers and farmers may build ponds to give their animals drinking water. Others may build ponds for raising fish. Some ponds and lakes also form when people build dams. Large lakes form when dams are built to provide a source of energy for producing electricity.

Ponds also form naturally. Just as rainwater collects in low-lying areas and forms puddles, larger amounts of water can collect and form a pond. The low-lying area may be land that has formed as layers of the Earth rose and fell.

When glaciers moved across North America during the last Ice Age, they hollowed out deep areas on the land's surface. In other places, the glaciers were trapped after carving out their path, came to a stop, and melted. As each glacier melted, it filled in these holes with water. Many large lakes and ponds formed in this way.

Directions → **Answer the questions in complete sentences. Use another sheet of paper for your answers.**

1. How is a pond like a puddle?

2. What are some reasons that people build ponds?

3. How do ponds form naturally?

Name _____   Date _____

How Water Forms a Delta

Have you ever walked along the bank of a mountain stream? The water looks so clear. When the water rushes down a stream, it picks up soil, sand, and bits of rock from the stream bed, or the bottom of the stream.

Over a long period of time, the water can even break up rock and wash it downstream. Whenever a river carves out its channel, it is carving out rock and soil.

In general, the faster the water flows, the more material it will pick up. When the water in the stream slows down, it drops some of the bits of soil, sand, and rock that it carries. Picking up and dropping off these tiny bits helps the river change its shape. The parts of the river that flow fast can dig out a new channel. Slower-moving parts of the river drop off material, building up new areas of land.

Bits of soil and rock are also dropped off when a river floods its banks. This drop-off of new material is good for plants. It makes them grow strong and healthy. So riverbanks are fertile—good places for growing crops and other plants.

Streams and rivers finally flow into the slow-moving waters of lakes or into the ocean. Most of the material that a river carries is dropped off right at its mouth. So much material is dropped off that it builds up a delta, a V-shaped area at its mouth. Deltas are very fertile areas.

Directions ➔ **Answer the questions in complete sentences. Use another sheet of paper for your answers.**

1. How does water change a river's shape?

2. Why are riverbanks fertile?

3. How are deltas formed?

Unit 3

How Rivers Form and Change

Directions ➡ Above each box is a description of one stage in the life of a river. In each box, draw a picture of the stage that is described. Draw a line from each label below the boxes to the part of the drawing that matches the label. Write a title for each of your drawings, telling which stage in the life of a river the drawing shows.

1. Falling rain and melting snow begin to run down a mountain. The flow of water becomes stronger and wider, and the water starts to carve out a channel as it flows. The channel becomes deeper and wider and is called a brook. When the brook flows deeper and faster, it gets larger and is called a stream. Other streams join the first stream to become a river.

Rainfall   **Brook**   **Streams join river**

Go on to the next page.

2. The river may tumble over a waterfall. That is where the land drops suddenly and the river falls over hard rock. When the river flows down a steep slope, whitewater rapids are formed by fast currents. As the river flows over a wide plain, it slows and curves. The curves form a lake.

Waterfalls   Rapids   Winding curves   Lake

3. The river flows into an ocean, bay, or gulf. It drops soil, sand, and rocks. It fans out at its mouth in the shape of a V. The V-shaped land is called a delta.

Delta

Pollution of Water

Have you ever wanted to go swimming and found that the beach was closed? Lakes and ponds sometimes become polluted. Then, for health and safety reasons, no swimming or boating is allowed. The pollution may be caused by a large number of bacteria living in the water. When these include a large number of bacteria that live in human or animal intestines, health workers worry. Not all bacteria that live in human or animal intestines are harmful, but some cause disease.

How do these bacteria get into the water? One way is that waste water could be leaking into the lake from a sewage plant or from a private septic system. During the summer, health workers take samples almost daily of water that is used for swimming.

Directions ➔ **Answer the questions.**

1. Why is it important to know if bacteria from sewage are present in water used for swimming and boating?

_____

_____

2. How can harmful bacteria enter the water in a lake or pond?

_____

_____

If there are more than 10,000 bacteria in 100 mL of water, health workers check to see how many of the bacteria come from human intestines. If there are more than 400 intestinal bacteria per 100 mL of water, the beaches surrounding the lake are closed. Health workers do not know for sure that there are harmful bacteria in the water. They do know that there is probably a leak of sewage into the lake.

Go on to the next page.

Name _____   Date _____

Pollution of Water, p. 2

Look at the graphs. They show the total daily bacterial count and the count of intestinal bacteria for a 10-day period.

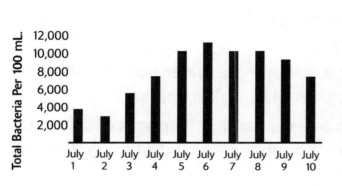

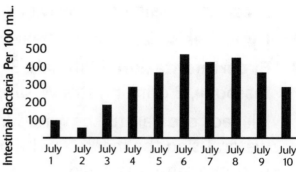

3. Why is it important to know the total number of bacteria present in a water sample? _____

_____

4. On which day(s) was the total count over 10,000 bacteria per 100 mL of water? _____

_____

5. On which day(s) was the intestinal bacteria count over 400 per mL of water? _____

_____

6. On which day(s) should the beach be closed?

_____

_____

Unit 3: Effects on the Environment
Water: Concepts and Applications, Gr. 3, SV 2709-X

Name _____   Date _____

Science Fair Ideas

A science fair project can help you to understand the world around you. Choose a topic that interests you. Then use the scientific method to develop your project. Here's an example:

1. **Problem:** Is salt water heavier than tap water?

2. **Hypothesis:** Salt water is heavier.

3. **Experimentation:** Materials: 3 paper cups, tap water, food coloring, teaspoon, 3 drinking straws, salt, clear plastic glass, marker

- Fill each cup half full of water. In one cup, add 2 teaspoons of salt to the water. Using the marker, write on the cup the amount of salt added. Stir until the salt is dissolved.

- Add 4 teaspoons of salt to another cup of water. Write the amount on the cup. Stir until the salt is dissolved. Leave one cup with no salt.

- Add a few drops of a different food coloring to each cup. Stir the water.

- Put a straw into the water that had 4 teaspoons of salt added. Put your finger over the opening, and move the straw over the clear plastic glass. Let the water run into the clear glass. Using another straw, repeat the process for the water containing 2 teaspoons of salt. Using another straw, repeat the process with the plain water.

4. **Observation:** The saltier water stayed on the bottom, the salty water stayed in the middle, and the plain tap water stayed on top.

5. **Conclusion:** Salty water is heavier than tap water.

6. **Comparison:** The conclusion and the hypothesis agree.

7. **Presentation:** Display the cup with the three layers of water.

8. **Resource:** Tell the books, magazines, or Internet sites you used for information. Tell who helped you to gather the resources and materials.

Other Project Ideas:

1. What happens to a steel-wool pad when it is left out in the rain?

2. What are some liquids that will or won't mix with water? Why do or don't they mix?